DOGS TO THE RESCUE!

SNOW SEARCH DOGS

By Sara Green

BELLWETHER MEDIA • MINNEAPOLIS, MN

Jump into the cockpit and take flight with *Pilot* books. Your journey will take you on high-energy adventures as you learn about all that is wild, weird, fascinating, and fun!

This edition first published in 2014 by Bellwether Media, Inc.

No part of this publication may be reproduced in whole or in part without written permission of the publisher. For information regarding permission, write to Bellwether Media, Inc., Attention: Permissions Department, 5357 Penn Avenue South, Minneapolis, MN 55419.

Library of Congress Cataloging-in-Publication Data

Green, Sara, 1964-
  Snow search dogs / by Sara Green.
    pages cm. – (Pilot: Dogs to the rescue!)
  Includes bibliographical references and index.
  Summary: "Engaging images accompany information about snow search dogs. The combination of high-interest subject matter and narrative text is intended for students in grades 3 through 7"–Provided by publisher.
  ISBN 978-1-60014-959-7 (hardcover : alk. paper)
  1. Search dogs–Juvenile literature. 2. Rescue dogs–Juvenile literature. 3. Avalanches–Juvenile literature. 4. Search and rescue operations–Juvenile literature. I. Title.
  SF428.73.G737 2014
  636.7'0886–dc23
                                2013009996

Printed in the United States of America, North Mankato, MN.

TABLE OF CONTENTS

A BRAVE RESCUE

Two skiers are halfway down a mountain. Suddenly, they hear a loud roar. They look up to see a huge mass of snow sliding toward them. This is an **avalanche**! The snow moves fast and covers everything in its path. The skiers do not have time to get away. Soon, they are buried deep in snow. Will they make it out alive?

A team of rescuers arrives at the scene as soon as possible. They bring a specially trained dog. Its **handler** gives a command. "Search!" The dog runs through the snow. It sniffs for the smell of humans. Within minutes, the dog gives a bark and begins to dig. The rescuers join in with shovels. Finally, they find one of the skiers. They pull him to safety. Soon, the dog starts to dig again. It has found the other skier. Both are safe thanks to this heroic dog!

5

WHAT ARE SNOW SEARCH DOGS?

Snow search dogs use their sense of smell to sniff for people lost or buried in the snow. These brave canines have been rescuing people for more than 200 years. The Saint Bernard was one of the first breeds used for snow rescues. These large dogs helped rescue people traveling through the Swiss Alps.

Today, a variety of other breeds are commonly used as snow search dogs. These include Border Collies, German Shepherds, Golden Retrievers, and Labrador Retrievers. Many snow search dogs are mixed breeds that come from shelters.

Saint Bernard

Breeds of Snow Search Dogs

Border Collie

German Shepherd

Golden Retriever

Labrador Retriever

Profile: Golden Retriever

Intelligence
The Golden Retriever is the fourth smartest dog breed. The dog will learn new commands with little repetition and will obey them almost every time.

Size
Height: 20 to 24 inches (51 to 61 centimeters)

Weight: 55 to 80 pounds (25 to 36 kilograms)

Sensitive Nose
The Golden Retriever has more than 200 million scent receptors in its nose. A human has only 5 million.

Snow search dogs must be fit, strong, and eager to learn. They must enjoy working with other dogs in snow and cold temperatures. Snow search dogs often work in busy ski areas. They must be friendly with people and remain calm when stress is high. The dogs also need to have **victim** loyalty. This means they stay with trapped victims until the rescue team arrives.

DEADLY AVALANCHES

Snow search dogs often rescue people who are caught in avalanches. Wind and high temperatures can trigger these massive snow slides, especially when the **snow pack** is weak. During an avalanche, the snow can **descend** at speeds of more than 80 miles (129 kilometers) per hour. Giant blocks of snow are left in the path of an avalanche. These blocks can be as large as trucks! When the snow stops moving, it may be as hard as cement.

Take Extra Care!

In the United States, most avalanches happen in January, February, and March. They occur most often in Alaska, Colorado, and Utah.

Avalanches can be deadly to victims buried in the hard snow. Victims are very cold and have little air to breathe. Many have broken bones or other injuries. Rescue workers must work quickly to find victims, but they often do not know where to look. Snow search dogs use their sensitive noses to locate these victims. With the help of snow search dogs, rescue workers can save many lives.

SEARCH AND RESCUE TRAINING

Dogs usually train for about two years to become snow search dogs. Training often begins when the dogs are puppies. First, they learn basic **obedience skills** and how to behave around people.

After they master basic skills, the dogs begin to learn search and rescue skills. In the first stage, dogs learn to find their handlers hiding in the snow. Dogs receive treats, praise, and other rewards when they find their handlers. Next, the dogs find strangers in the snow and receive more rewards. This way, the dogs learn that finding someone in the snow is a fun game!

Snow search dogs learn to sniff for people in all types of weather. They learn to ignore food, snowmobiles, and noisy crowds while they are on the job. After they complete their training, the dogs receive **certification**. Now they are ready to respond to a real snow emergency!

People who are caught in avalanches are often buried several feet down. Snow search dogs use air scenting to find victims. When people are trapped in snow, their scent rises through the snow and into the air. The dogs sniff the air to find where this scent is the strongest. When the dogs smell a person, they bark and begin to dig in the snow. This alerts the rescue workers that the dog has found an avalanche victim.

After dogs give an alert, rescue workers **probe** the area with long poles. This allows them to pinpoint the victim's exact location in the snow. Now the rescue workers must use shovels to quickly dig the victim out of the snow. The dogs also continue to dig. After the victim is out of the snow, the dogs are rewarded with playtime. They have done their job well!

probing

Outstanding Sniffers

Dogs can easily sniff victims trapped in up to 15 feet (4.6 meters) of snow. Many can even smell people buried much deeper. One European snow search dog found someone trapped under 39 feet (12 meters) of snow!

A DEDICATED TEAM

Snow search dogs and their handlers live, work, and play together. They learn to trust each other and understand each other's signals. This teamwork helps them act quickly in emergencies. Handlers must be strong and fit to hike and ski over difficult **terrain**. These snow safety experts have avalanche awareness skills and advanced first aid training.

Many snow search dogs and their handlers work at ski resorts as members of the ski patrol. Snow search dogs usually wear special vests. They have a cross and the word *rescue* on them. The vests help people recognize which dogs are on duty. Every day, the dogs ride chairlifts to get to the top of the ski runs. From up there, snow search dogs are ready to go wherever they are needed.

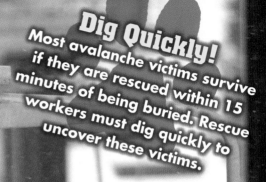

Dig Quickly!

Most avalanche victims survive if they are rescued within 15 minutes of being buried. Rescue workers must dig quickly to uncover these victims.

Snow search dogs and their handlers usually participate in 2 to 10 rescues each winter. Most avalanches occur in the **backcountry**. People sometimes ski, snowboard, or ride snowmobiles in areas where the avalanche risk is high. Victims may not be able to call for help. For this reason, rescue teams often check the backcountry after an avalanche to make sure that nobody was buried.

Snow search dogs travel to rescue sites in a variety of ways. They often travel by helicopter, snowmobile, or sled. This allows them to get to **remote** areas quickly. Sometimes, handlers carry the dogs on their shoulders. They do this when they enter deep snow or steep terrain. The dogs also learn to run behind the skis of their handlers. This protects them from running into the skis' sharp edges.

Avalanche Prevention

Many ski resorts have avalanche control teams. They use explosives to trigger small avalanches on mountains before skiers arrive. This helps prevent larger avalanches from occurring later.

17

AN ACTIVE LIFE

Snow search dogs remain active even when they are not participating in rescues. Every day, they practice with their handlers to keep their skills sharp. They also enjoy playing in the snow with people and other dogs. Some snow search dogs and their handlers visit schools. They teach children about mountain safety. Many participate in educational programs at ski resorts. **Tourists** meet the dogs and learn about avalanche safety.

Snow search dogs usually **retire** when they are between 7 and 10 years old. Most retired dogs live with their handlers. Sometimes the handlers cannot take care of them. Then the dogs are adopted by loving families. After years of dedicated service, the dogs enjoy lives filled with fun, games, and rest!

BARRY: THE MOUNTAIN DOG

In the early 1800s, a Saint Bernard named Barry became a famous rescue dog. Barry lived in a **monastery** high in the mountains of Switzerland. In those days, people had to cross the mountains on horseback or by foot. Many faced great dangers from the snow and cold. The paths were snowy most of the year, which made travel difficult. The **monks** trained Saint Bernards to rescue people.

Barry was among the bravest of the dogs. He saved the lives of more than 40 people. One of his greatest rescues happened on an icy ledge. There, Barry found a young boy fast asleep and covered in snow. Barry lay on top of the boy and licked his face to warm him. When the boy woke up, he climbed on Barry's back. The heroic dog carried the boy safely back to the monastery. Today, people remember Barry as one of the greatest rescue dogs of all time.

GLOSSARY

avalanche—a massive snow slide

backcountry—wilderness areas

certification—the process that recognizes that a dog has mastered specific job skills

descend—to go down

handler—a person who is responsible for a highly trained dog

monastery—a place where people live to commit their lives to their religion

monks—men who live in monasteries

obedience skills—skills such as sit, stay, down, and come

probe—to explore something with a hand or tool

remote—far away from a town or city

retire—to stop working

snow pack—a layer of snow

terrain—a stretch of land

tourists—people who travel to visit another place

victim—a person who is harmed or killed in a tragic event or natural disaster

TO LEARN MORE

AT THE LIBRARY

Miller, Marie-Therese. *Search and Rescue Dogs*. New York, N.Y.: Chelsea Clubhouse, 2007.

Rajczak, Kristen. *Rescue Dogs*. New York, N.Y.: Gareth Stevens Publishing, 2011.

Silverman, Maida. *Snow Search Dogs*. New York, N.Y.: Bearport Pub., 2006.

ON THE WEB

Learning more about snow search dogs is as easy as 1, 2, 3.

1. Go to www.factsurfer.com.

2. Enter "snow search dogs" into the search box.

3. Click the "Surf" button and you will see a list of related Web sites.

With factsurfer.com, finding more information is just a click away.

INDEX